T0131819

ISH FISH
and the
WISH

Lorena Burnett

AuthorHouse™
1663 Liberty Drive
Bloomington, IN 47403
www.authorhouse.com
Phone: 833-262-8899

This book is printed on acid-free paper.

ISBN: 978-1-6655-7899-8 (sc)
ISBN: 978-1-6655-7900-1 (e)

Print information available on the last page.

Published by AuthorHouse 12/22/2022

authorHOUSE®

ISH FISH
and the
WISH

The Strange Noise

Dump, Illinois, a town known for its haunted houses lined up on the shady riverbank. One night something happened that Ish would never forget. It was in the wee hours of August 13, 2004, at 2:25 a.m., the darkest night of the fisher boy's life. He heard footsteps coming from the downstairs hallway. Ish pretended to be fast asleep; he didn't even open his eyelids.

MARIA MCBRIDE

Creak, creak, creak went the strange noise. There was a dim nightlight on the wall near Ish's bed because he was afraid of the dark, which caused him to have nightmares and horrible dreams. These were especially bad when he watched his favorite horror video game which his Mom and Dad had forbidden him from watching it. Ish justified his actions because he saved his very own money, and his older friend had purchased it for him.

Ish thought, *It must be the ghost of the night.* He pulled the blue blanket his mom had knitted for him tight over his head as to block out the strange noise. Ish sometimes found himself on the floor on the blue carpet after wrestling in his sleep. *Squeak, squeak* went the creepy sound; the noise came closer and closer to Ish's bedroom door. Suddenly there was silence; the door opened just a crack, and that was when Ish smelled the scent of shaving cream.

Wow! It Was Only Dad

Wow, it's only Dad, Ish thought, *making sure I'm safe and tucked underneath my blue blanket.* Dad tiptoed into Ish's bedroom; he gently tucked the blue blanket around Ish's warm body, and then he tiptoed out of the room. After Ish heard the bedroom door close, he peeked his head out from underneath the blue blanket. Then he remembered it was his birthday—August 13.

The Special Gift

Ish was faithful in carrying the trash to the curb for the garbage truck without being asked. He had been keeping his bedroom tidy, and Mom had not tripped over any of his toys. He had been doing his homework immediately when he came home from school, before he watched any videos or turned on the television to play his favorite games. He also went to bed on time without fussing.

Ish was very curious; he could hardly wait until morning to open the special birthday gift Mom and Dad had bought for him. *My special present must be in a special place,* Ish thought. He tumbled out of bed and put on his favorite socks, the ones with heavy padding. They were soundproof so that no one could hear creepy sounds when he walked across the floor. Ish tiptoed across the hallway and down the staircase, where he heard the creepy sound coming from earlier.

The closet door was cracked just a little; Ish found his favorite stepstool and climbed on the very top step. Then he opened the big closet door. What do you think Ish saw? His eyes became big as saucers as he stared into the closet.

He saw a huge box wrapped with paper in his favorite colors—blue, yellow, and white. The wrapping paper had birthday balloons with fish designs on it of various shapes and sizes. A piece of rectangular paper hung from the package from a ribbon, and the note on it read, "A birthday surprise for our little fisher boy. Love, Mom and Dad." Ish did not have to tear a hole in the wrapper paper to take a small peek; he knew exactly what the gift was.

Giving Thanks

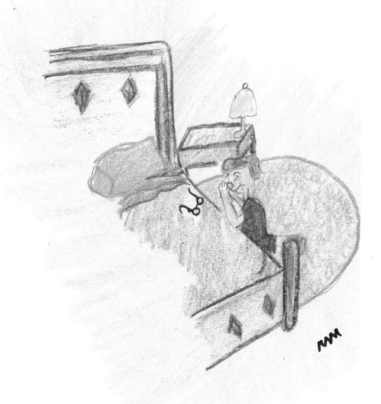

Ish gently closed the closet door so Mom and Dad would not wake from their peaceful sleep. He boldly tiptoed up the staircase and down the dark hallway, murmuring, "I am not afraid of the ghost of the night." Then he knelt beside his bed and thanked his heavenly Father for his mom and dad, who would be giving his special gift. Then he climbed into his bed and made a wish.

Ish and the Wish

I wish, I wish, thought Ish as he fell fast asleep. He was so thrilled about his birthday gift that his dream that night was pleasant instead of the usual nightmare. Ish dreamed he was on the shady riverbank in Dump, Illinois. His legs were crossed, his bare feet rested in the dirt, his T-shirt sat on a stump, and in his hand was his special birthday gift—a fishing pole. He also had a can of wiggly worms to use as bait.

I wish, I wish, thought Ish, *that I could catch a great big fish on my ninth birthday. Dad would be so proud of me.* Ish imagined relatives coming to the house for a big fish fry. *I am so thrilled. Now I know I am a big fisher boy, because I will catch my very own fish. I will never, never, never stop fishing.*

Then he thought, *I wish, I wish I could swim like a fish. I would swim over to Riverboat Town to Grandma and Grandpa's riverboat home. I would swim all day and night; I will never, never stop swimming.*

Obey Your Parents

Splish, splash went the water as the plump fish swam by. Fish saw Wiggly Worm on the hook crying, "Help me, help me! Somebody please help me!"

"Did he say help myself?" Fish murmured. "I sure will." Fish knew this was his supper, perhaps his only meal for the day. He looked up through the sky of the foggy water; he could see a boy sitting on a tree stump near the riverbank. The boy was relaxed and smiling, with his bare feet and legs crossed and a can of Wiggly Worm's family on the ground. In his hand the boy had a fishing pole connected to a silver line.

Fish then remembered what his momma and poppa fish taught him. "Son, when you look up through a foggy sky of the water and see a shadow of a pole, a silver line, and a wiggly worm on a hook, forget that dinner, or you will be the dinner. Just swim on by."

Fish imagined hearing his momma fish singing, "Obey your parents," and his poppa fish with his Bible praying: "Swim on by." Fish knew he would have hunger pains that day, but he would still be alive if he obeyed his parents and the Lord. Do you sometimes have hungry pain when you miss a meal?

I wish, I wish, thought Fish as he dosed into an unfulfilled dream, *I wish I was the boy relaxing on the riverbank tree stump and that he was me, a hungry fish in the water. Then I would put that crying wiggly worm on a hook and catch myself a dinner. I wouldn't want to be a wiggly worm, though, because he is such a crybaby.*

You would cry too, thought Wiggly Worm, *if you were on a hook dangling for a fish dinner.*

Wiggly Worm continued to cry. He cried and cried until his tears formed as a huge group of waves in the river. The waves felt sorry for Wiggly Worm, and they began to cry as well. The water was angry as it began to rise; the current in the water became stronger, and soon the water overflowed onto the riverbank. What do you think happened then?

Oh! What's wrong with this picture? Have you ever wished for something that maybe came out the wrong way? Could this imaginary dream ever come true? How would you feel if you were a hungry fish waiting for a wiggly worm to be caught for your dinner? How would you feel if you were a wiggly worm serving as fish bait? What do you think Ish thought as he was fishing and waiting for a fish dinner?

The water rose so high that Wiggly Worm came off the hook and landed on the bank of the river. He shouted, "Free! I'm free! Freedom!"

The waves were so strong that Fish went sailing through the air, almost touching the angry cloud; he landed on the riverbank where Ish was fishing. "Yahoo! Yahoo!" shouted Fish.

The angry waves were so forceful that they pulled Ish down into the river until he was caught on the line like Wiggly Worm had been. "Help me! Help me! Somebody please help me," cried Ish.

Did everyone get their wish? Where was everyone? Fish was on the riverbank, fishing with the fishing pole. Wiggly Worm was on the riverbank, free and with his family. And Ish was on the hook at the end of the silver line, serving as bait.

Only a Horrible Dream

Ish was crying in his sleep. "Help! Help! Somebody please help me!" He cried so loud that his dad awoke from a peaceful sleep. Dad jumped out of bed and ran as fast as his legs could carry him toward Ish's bedroom. Ish felt his body shaking.

"Wake up! Wake up, son!" shouted Dad. Ish's pajamas were soaked with sweat. "Wake up," Dad said gently.

Ish tumbled out of bed. "What is this?" murmured Ish. "Is this the ghost of the wind on the river? No! It's my dad shaking me out of a horrible dream. Today is our fishing trip."

"And your special day," said Dad.

Ish went to the stairway and tiptoed down the steps. Mom was waiting for him; she had baked a big birthday cake in a form of a fish.

Ish looked in the corner of the kitchen and saw a huge box wrapped with blue, yellow, and white, wrapping paper; he quickly tore the wrapping paper off the box. When he opened the box and saw a fishing pole, he shrugged.

"What is wrong with you, Ish?" his dad said. "You have been waiting for your special birthday gift for a long time."

"Yes, Dad," replied Ish. "I know, but I had a horrible dream about fishing."

"Well, son, tell me about your dream."

So, Ish said, "What if you were a fish and someone put a crying wiggly worm on a hook to trap you for a fish dinner?"

"So that's what's bothering you. It's time we have a father-and-son talk. We must be who we are; we are all here for a specific purpose. Wiggly worms are here to be bait for the fish. The wiggly worms would rather be the fish, so they could have a better chance to swim away and not be dinner, but this is not meant to be.

There is a king who owns the universe; he is divine. You cannot see him, but you can believe in him and feel His presence. He came down from heaven to be with us on earth and to give himself to us. He is our food, our sacrifice—just like the fish is our food and sacrifice. The wiggly worms are the fish's food and sacrifice."Ish said, "The king must be the invisible man."

"Yes! He is in every Christian heart. He once was a little boy just like you. He also loved to fish."

"Did his wiggly worms cry?"

"Yes! But his wiggly worms are you and me and all the world. When the world found out who he was and what he had done for them, their hearts were sad, and they were sorry for their wrongdoing. They cried great big tears, just like the crying wiggly worm and the angry waves."

"What should I call him?" Ish asked.

"His name is Jesus, and he came from heaven to earth to save us from our wrongdoing. We did not understand him because we did not know him, but he loves us the same. He died and was buried, but he came back to life."

"Will the fish and the wiggly worm come back to life too?"

"Only Jesus has the answer. He promised to come back when we die and take us to our new home, heaven, to live with him forever. His commandment is children obey their parents in the Lord and that parents should obey him."

After reading this story, should we be careful what we wish for?

Ephesians 6:1–3 (KJV): "Children obey your parent in the Lord for this is right. Honor your father and mother, which is the first commandment with promise that it may be well with thee, and thou may live long on the earth."

The Wiggles Have a Plan

Mr. and Mrs. Wiggly Worm have a plan. See how the Wiggles taught their little worms to have no worries or stress.

"Listen, my little ones," said Mr. Wiggly Worm. "The ground is moist, and this day our home will be destroyed. It is fishing season, and the fishermen will dig us out of our cozy beds. We will be put on their hooks as bait for fish; The fishermen and their families will consume the fish. Then one day the fishermen will also be destroyed.

"Don't be afraid, for we will rise again. Relax—the journey begins with us," said Mrs. Wiggly Worm. The little worm family laughed, danced, and wiggled as they waited patiently to be dug up from the ground.

The fishermen arrived. Knowing their dinner would be taken, Mr. and Mrs. Robin Bird tweeted a distressed sound from their favorite tree, cuddling their little family as they watched the fishermen walking toward the moist ground where the worm families were asleep.

"That's not the proper way to catch a fish," shouted Hix.

Bubba had a sling with a huge rock in it, leaning forward so he could hit the fish as it swam in the water. Hix was standing close to the water and giggling; he could not hardly wait to see the fish's reaction after he hit it on the head. Would it knock him out, wondered Bubba and Hix, or would it just make him dizzy?

Ish ran to catch up with his buddies, hollering, "Hey, guys, I got a large can of wiggly worms; want to share with me?" Ish then stopped in surprise; what he saw made him very upset. "Hey," said Ish, "that is not the proper way to catch fish."

"Who says!" shouted Bubba. "Where is the rule book that says you must catch fish a certain way?"

"Well," says Ish, "Let me tell you a story of my experience, and just maybe you will learn from it."

Ish, Bubba, and Hix sat on a huge log as the worms wiggled in the can. Ish told his story about the angry waves and how he traded places with the wiggly worm and was the hook, scared and trembling; he also shared the fate of the fish. He learned that everything comes with a price; he told them the story of Jesus as his dad told him and explained that we should not abuse our talents or gifts and the way we get the food that Jesus gives to us. Hix and Bubba listened with sad hearts; puddles of water fell from their eyes. Teardrops also rushed down Ish's face, for he knew they would be buddies forever.

The End

Activities: Draw and Color

Each character has his or her own identity. Draw and color the characters.

Ish

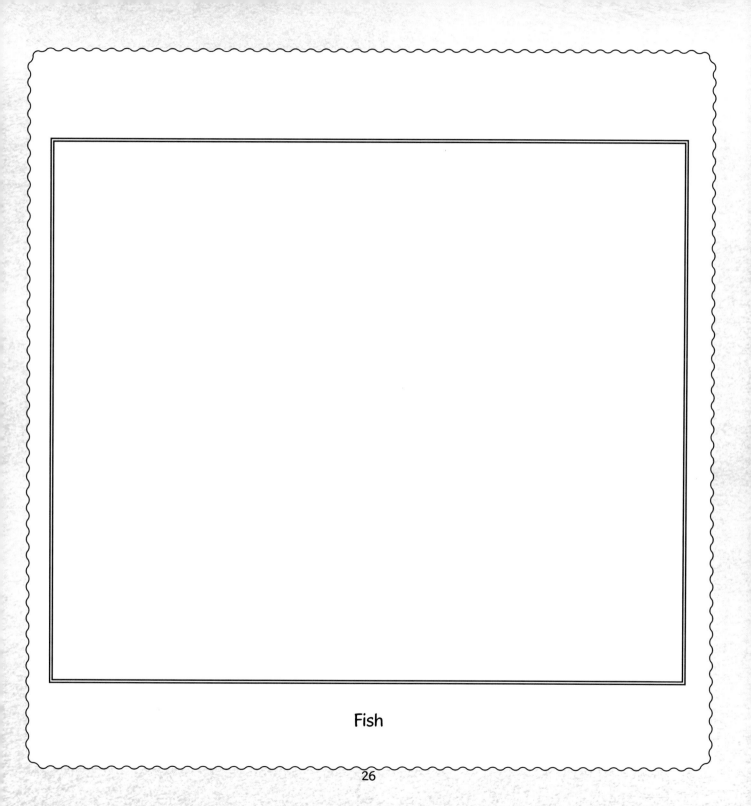

Fish

Wiggly Worm

Bubba

Hix

About the Author

Lorena Burnett was born in the town of Metropolis, Illinois. She is a divorcée and the mother of five sons. She has daughters-in-law, grandchildren, great-grandchildren, and godchildren. She has three sisters and seven brothers. When Lorena was young, her mother relocated to Alton, Illinois, where Lorena attended public schools. She worked at Olin Corporation from 1976 to 2008. She holds an associate of arts degree in early childhood education.

She is the founder and president of the nonprofit organization the Gift of God Ministries, where she works with the deaf youth (1995–2022). Her day-to-day responsibilities include speaking on a local radio station, KSTL 690 AM. She is an ordained evangelist, recording artist, poet, and dreamer, and she has the gift of prophecy. Her hobbies are writing and singing. She is the author of the *book Nobody but YOU, Lord* and future children's books.

lbgogmin@hotmail.com
P.O. Box 492
East Alton IL 62024
Future Book by Lorena Burnett
Eager Beaver